Jesus Saves!

Take-Home Mini-Books

by

Sandy Wardman

Carson-Dellosa Publishing Company, Inc.
Greensboro, North Carolina

Credits

It is the mission of Carson-Dellosa Christian Education to create the highest-quality Scripture-based children's products that teach the Word of God, share His love and goodness, assist in faith development, and glorify His Son, Jesus Christ.

"... teach me your ways so I may know you. ..."
Exodus 33:13

To Kayla and Ashley Prendergast
and their talented mother, Kelly Prendergast,
who provided invaluable help with the craft ideas.

Thanks to critique partners
Carole Frankel and Elaine Thiel.

Editor .... Pamela Holley-Bright
Layout Design .... Clint Moore
Inside Illustrations ..... Erik Huffine
Cover Design .... Peggy Jackson
Cover Illustrations ..... Erik Huffine

Unless otherwise noted, all Scripture is taken from the HOLY BIBLE, NEW INTERNATIONAL VERSION®. Copyright © 1973, 1978, 1984 by International Bible Society. Used by permission of Zondervan Bible Publishers.

Scripture quotations marked NLT are taken from the Holy Bible, New Living Translation, copyright 1996. Used by permission of Tyndale House Publishers, Inc., Wheaton, Illinois 60189. All rights reserved.

Printed in the USA • All rights reserved.   ISBN 978-1-60022-440-9

Table of Contents

How to Use This Book

Jesus Saves! features 12 easy-to-prepare lessons on the words and works of Jesus. A paraphrased take-home mini-book is the centerpiece of each lesson and is supplemented with discussion, craft, and puzzle activities.

Each lesson includes:

- **PREPARE YOUR HEART** This is a short encouraging meditation to prepare your heart to teach the material. Scripture passages are introduced to reflect on the meaning of the lesson. Writing your thoughts and feelings in a journal is encouraged.

- **LET'S BEGIN** This section includes a warm-up activity with discussion questions and ideas for class participation. Preview the Items Needed lists each week in case you choose to ask children to bring supplies from home for these activities.

- **LET'S LISTEN** Create the mini-book in advance and read it to the class. Then, provide each child with a mini-book to color and construct. The last page of each mini-book contains a note to parents, suggested follow-up activities for home, and the Bible references for the stories told in the mini-book.

Making the mini-book is simple. First, make one-sided copies of the mini-book pages. Place each page in the center of the copying space rather than against the edge. Next, color the pages and cut the pages in half along the dashed lines. Finally, turn the pages in the same direction, check that they are in the correct order, and staple the pages together. You may also choose to use a hole-punch and bind the pages with yarn or ribbon.

- **LET'S CREATE** Create the craft in advance and show it to the class. Provide children with supplies and help them to create the craft. Preview the Items Needed lists each week in case you choose to ask children to bring supplies from home for these crafts. Each craft includes an extension activity if time allows.

- **LET'S PUZZLE** Each lesson includes a fun puzzle worksheet. It can be used in class or sent home as supplemental material.

- **LET'S REVIEW AND PRAY** This section includes a quick review and a short prayer to conclude the lesson.

Jesus Is Born!

❧ Prepare Your Heart ❧

Therefore the Lord himself will give you a sign: The virgin will be with child and will give birth to a son, and will call him Immanuel. Isaiah 7:14

But you, Bethlehem Ephrathah, though you are small among the clans of Judah, out of you will come for me one who will be ruler over Israel, whose origins are from of old, from ancient times. Micah 5:2

These verses from the prophets are quoted in the Gospels. They show us that God has always had a plan for the salvation of His people. He promised His people that He would send them a ruler—a Savior—and He kept His promise.

Write a list of all of God's promises that you can recall. Take a moment to thank God for keeping all of His promises to you. The *Jesus Is Born!* lesson shows how the Lord kept his promise by sending His son. Ask God to prepare your heart to teach children about the gift of His precious Son, Jesus Christ.

❧ Let's Begin ❧

Items Needed

- One copy of the song "Away in a Manger"

- Pieces of a Nativity scene

Distribute a piece of the Nativity scene to each child. Nativity characters can be made by wrapping craft sticks with pieces of cloth. Nativity animals can be drawn, decorated, and then cut out and placed on craft sticks. Let children take turns placing their pieces around the manger and telling which character each piece represents. Sing "Away in a Manger" when all of the pieces have been placed in the scene.

❧ Let's Listen ❧

1. Photocopy and cut the *Jesus Is Born!* mini-book (pages 6–10) so that you have a set for each child in the class and an extra set for a sample book.

2. Read the *Jesus Is Born!* mini-book to the class.

3. Distribute a mini-book to each child. While children are coloring the pages, engage them with the following questions:

   - God promised to send someone to save us. Can anyone tell me whom God sent?

   - Why do we celebrate Christmas?

   - What is your favorite activity during Christmastime? Ask each child to share.

   - How does your family celebrate Christmas? Ask each child to share.

JESUS IS BORN!

The angel of the Lord appeared to Joseph in a dream and said, "Take Mary home as your wife. She will give birth to a son. Name him Jesus. He will save many people."
Joseph obeyed the angel of the Lord.

6

God loves us. God kept His promise and sent us His son.

Joseph and Mary traveled to Bethlehem. There was no room in the inn.
So, Joseph and Mary stayed in a stable.
When Jesus was born, they wrapped Him in cloths and placed Him in a manger.

God loves us. God kept His promise and sent His son. **4**

An angel appeared to nearby shepherds and said, "Today, a Savior is born."
Then, more angels appeared before the shepherds. Praising God, they said,
"Glory to God in the highest."
The shepherds went to see the baby.

5

God loves us. God kept His promise and sent His son. **6**

Magi from the East followed a bright star to Nazareth and found Jesus. The Magi gave gifts to Jesus. They said, "We want to worship the King of the Jews." **7**

God loves us. God kept His promise and sent His son.

8

✿ Note to Parents ✿

Today, your child learned how the birth of Jesus brought about the fulfillment of many of God's promises and that God always keeps His promises. We learned about the visit of the shepherds and the Magi. We also learned that when we celebrate Jesus' birth, we are celebrating God's love and faithfulness in His promise to send a Savior. Remind your child of this promise and why we celebrate Christmas.

Activities for Home

1. Ask your child about his favorite activities during Christmastime.

2. Explain to your child how some of your family's Christmas traditions began.

3. Act out the Nativity story with family members.

4. Sing Christmas songs. In class, your child sang "Away in a Manger."

5. God kept his promise and sent His son. Read these stories in:
   Matthew 1:18–25; Luke 2:4–7, 2:8–20; Matthew 2:1–12

9

ꙮ Let's Create ꙮ
── Items Needed ──

- One copy of the Birth Announcement Pattern (page 12) for each child

- Scissors, glue, and crayons or felt pens

- List of each child's birth date

- Magazines for cutting out pictures

1. Prepare and decorate a sample Birth Announcement (page 12) with your own birth date.

2. Show the class your sample birth announcement. Ask whether any children have newborns in their family. Did their parents send out birth announcements?

3. Distribute copies of the blank Birth Announcement Pattern (page 12). Help each child fill in his name and birth date.

4. Instruct children to find and cut out pictures that show character traits about themselves or things that they like, such as pets, sports, friends, or family. Have children paste the pictures on their birth announcements.

Extension Activity

Sit in a circle. Let each child show his certificate and announce his birth date to the class. Encourage children to share their character traits or the things that they like.

ꙮ Let's Puzzle ꙮ

Photocopy the A"maze"ing Magi worksheet (page 13) for each child. Use in class or as a take-home sheet. Remind children that while most Nativity scenes show the Magi at the manger, the Magi did not find Jesus until he was about 18 months old and living in a house in Nazareth. (Matthew 2:11)

ꙮ Let's Review and Pray ꙮ

1. Review the events of Jesus' birth.

2. Sing "Away in a Manger."

3. Say this prayer:

   Father God, thank You for the birth of Your Son, Jesus. Thank You for keeping Your promises. Help us to learn about Jesus. Help us to know Him better. In the name of your Son, Jesus Christ. Amen.

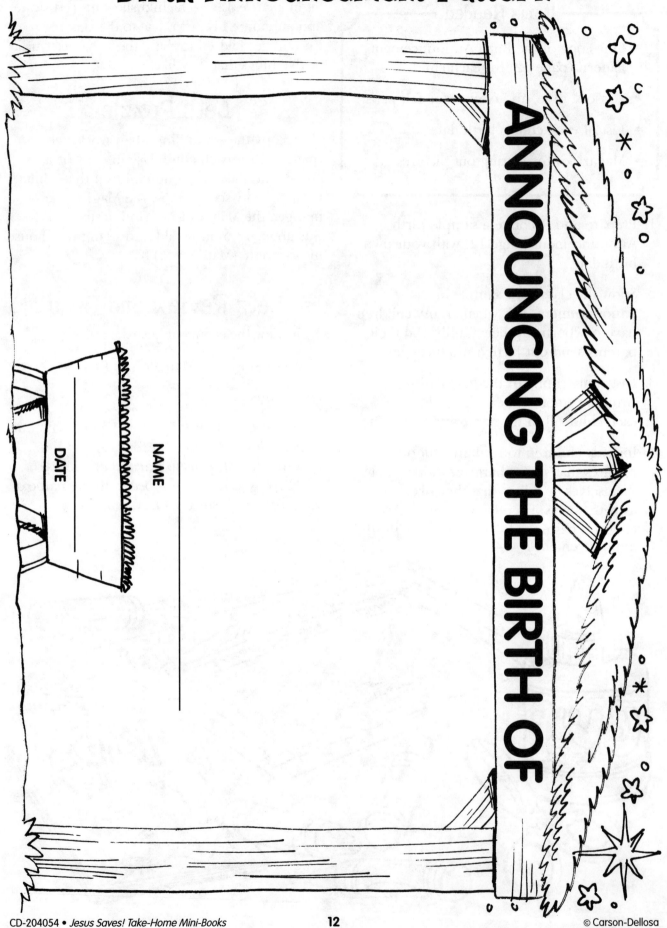

ANNOUNCING THE BIRTH OF

NAME

DATE

A"maze"ing Magi

Directions: Follow the maze to help the Magi find Jesus.

START

FINISH

"On coming to the house, they saw the child with his
mother Mary, and they bowed down and worshiped him."

Matthew 2:11

Jesus Saves! Take-Home Mini-Books • CD-204054

Jesus Loves His Family and Friends

❧ Prepare Your Heart ❧

Wives, submit to your husbands, as is fitting in the Lord. Husbands, love your wives and do not be harsh with them. Children, obey your parents in everything, for this pleases the Lord. Fathers, do not embitter your children, or they will become discouraged. Colossians 3:18–21

'. . . honor your father and mother,' and 'love your neighbor as yourself.' Matthew 19:19

Think about your family and friends. What are some of the ways that you show your love for them? We are commanded by God to love our families and to love each other. The following lesson will show examples of how Jesus loved His family and His friends and how we should love, too.

❧ Let's Begin ❧

─ Items Needed ─

- Photos of your family and friends

- Children's photos of their friends or families

1. Sit in a circle or group. Share the photos of your friends and families.

2. Have children take turns sharing information or photos of their friends or families.

❧ Let's Listen ❧

1. Photocopy and cut the *Jesus Loves His Family and Friends* mini-book (pages 15–19) so that you have a set for each child in the class and an extra set for a sample book.

2. Read the *Jesus Loves His Family and Friends* mini-book to the class.

3. Distribute a mini-book to each child. While children are coloring the pages, engage them with the following questions:

- How do you know that your parents love you? What things do they do to show their love?

- Have you ever been lost from your parents? How did you feel when they found you?

- Do you play with your brother or sister? What do you do together?

- Why do you love your friends? What ways can you show them that you love them?

JESUS LOVES HIS FAMILY AND FRIENDS

CD-204054 • *Jesus Saves! Take-Home Mini-Books*

When Jesus was 12 years old, He traveled to Jerusalem with His family for the Feast of the Passover. His parents worried when they couldn't find Jesus among the crowds.

When they found him in the Temple, Jesus said, "I had to be in my Father's house. I will come with you to Nazareth. I will obey you."

Mary and Joseph loved Jesus. Jesus loved His family.

"Jesus, your mother and brothers are outside looking for you."
Jesus asked, "Who is my mother, and who are my brothers? Whoever does the
will of my Father is my brother and sister and mother."

Jesus' brothers and sisters loved Him. Jesus loved His family.

Jesus walked into Simon Peter's house. He saw Simon Peter's mother-in-law lying in bed with a fever. Jesus touched her hand, and the fever went away. She got up and fixed Jesus something to eat.

Simon Peter loved Jesus. Jesus loved His friends.

6

After Jesus died, His friend Mary Magdalene went to the tomb. She saw two angels, but Jesus' body was gone.
"Who is it you are looking for?" a voice behind her asked.
She turned around and saw Jesus standing in the garden. She ran to Him.

7

Mary Magdalene loved Jesus. Jesus loved His friends.

8

🎀 Note to Parents 🎀

Jesus showed us how to love through loving His friends and His family. Jesus commanded us to honor our fathers and mothers and to love our neighbors as ourselves. (Matthew 19:19) In today's lesson, your child discovered ways that Jesus loved His friends and His family. She also learned ways that she can show love for her family and friends. What are some of the ways that you show your love for your family and friends?

Activities for Home

1. Talk to your child about the day he was born. What were you doing when labor started? Which family members were there? How did you select your child's name?

2. Take out a family photo album and talk with your child about the family members in the pictures. Have your child send a card to a family member who lives far away.

3. Have your child invite a friend over to play.

4. Jesus loved His family and friends. Read these stories in:
   Luke 2:41–52; Matthew 12:46–50, 8:14–15; John 20:11–18

❧ Let's Create ❧

Items Needed

- One copy of the Heart Patterns (page 21) on colorful construction paper for each child

- Photograph of each child

- Old compact discs (one per child)

- Scissors, glue, craft sticks

1. Prepare a sample compact disc flower.

2. Photograph each child or have children bring in photographs of themselves.

3. Distribute one page of the Heart Patterns (page 21) on colorful construction paper to each child.

4. Help children cut out the hearts. Or, have precut hearts available for children who may have difficulty cutting.

5. Instruct children to glue the pointed part of the hearts onto the non-shiny sides of the compact discs to make the petals of the flowers.

6. Have children paste their photos on the shiny sides of the compact discs.

7. Instruct children to attach the craft sticks to complete their flowers.

Extension Activity

Sing the song "Jesus Loves the Little Children" with children. Have them march around the room waving their flowers as they sing.

❧ Let's Puzzle ❧

Photocopy the Around Jerusalem worksheet (page 22) for each child. Use in class or as a take-home sheet.

❧ Let's Review and Pray ❧

1. Have children stand in a circle and hold hands.

2. Each child should tell the person to her right something that she likes about him.

3. Say this prayer:

Dear Father God, please show us ways that we can be like You and show love to our family and friends. In the name of Your Son, Jesus Christ. Amen.

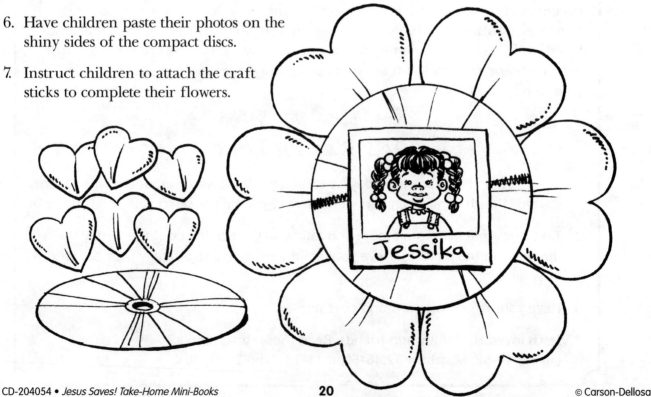

✿ Heart Patterns ✿

❧ Around Jerusalem ❧

Directions: Search to find Jesus in Jerusalem. Color the picture.

DOVES FOR SALE

MONEY CHANG

"After three days they found him in the temple courts,
sitting among the teachers, listening to them and asking them questions."
Luke 2:46

Jesus Works Miracles
❧ Prepare Your Heart ❧

"The miracles I do in my Father's name speak for me . . . believe the miracles, that you may know and understand that the Father is in me, and I in the Father." John 10:25, 38

"Have faith in God. . . . whatever you ask for in prayer, believe that you have received it, and it will be yours." Mark 11:22, 24

During Jesus' lifetime on Earth, He performed many miracles. He performed them so that the people would believe that He was indeed God's Son. Today, we can still see the miracles of Jesus through healing, provision, and the miracle of changed lives and hearts. Sit quietly and think about the miracles that you saw this past week. Write them down and thank God for His hand in your life.

❧ Let's Begin ❧

1. Children are seated. Give the following commands and have them sit down after each one:

    • Stand up if you know someone who was sick and is now better.

    • Stand up if someone loves you very much.

    • Stand up if you have a family.

    • Stand up if you have seen beautiful flowers.

    • Stand up if you have seen a newborn baby.

2. Explain to children that these are all miracles of God's love and that God loves them very much.

3. Help them understand what miracles are. Explain that they are wonderful events that show God's love and power.

❧ Let's Listen ❧

1. Photocopy and cut the *Jesus Works Miracles* mini-book (pages 24–28) so that you have a set for each child in the class and an extra set for a sample book.

2. Read the *Jesus Works Miracles* mini-book to the class.

3. Distribute a mini-book to each child. While children are coloring the pages, engage them with the following questions:

    • Who has seen a miracle this week? Can you tell us what you saw? List the miracles that the children mention.

    • Why does Jesus work miracles for us? (Because He never changes. He loves us and responds to faith, just as he did when He was on Earth.)

JESUS WORKS MIRACLES

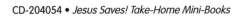

Jesus and His mother, Mary, went to a wedding.
"They have no more wine," Mary said.
"Fill the jars with water and give some to the head of the banquet," Jesus said.
A servant poured out the water and said, "The water has turned into wine!"

2

Jesus worked a miracle for His friends. Jesus will work miracles for you. **2**

While Jesus was praying on a mountainside, the disciples were in a boat on a lake. The wind blew and made big waves.
A disciple shouted, "Look! Jesus is walking on the water."
Jesus said, "Do not be afraid." He climbed into the boat with the disciples. **3**

Jesus worked a miracle for His friends. Jesus will work miracles for you.   **4**

Peter entered the house. "Jesus, we have to pay the Temple tax."
Jesus said, "Go to the sea; look in the mouth of the first fish that you catch."
Peter caught the fish and opened its mouth. "Look, a coin to pay the tax!"   **5**

Jesus worked a miracle for His friends. Jesus will work miracles for you. **6**

"We haven't caught a single fish," Peter said.
Jesus stood on the shore. "Throw out your net one more time," He said.
"Now, the net is full," the disciples said.
John looked at Jesus. "You are the Lord. You filled the net with fish."

7

Jesus worked a miracle for His friends. Jesus will work miracles for you. **8**

Note to Parents

Today, your child learned about some of the miracles that Jesus performed. Your child also learned that Jesus never changes and that miracles still happen today. We see the miracles of Jesus through healing, provision and the miracle of changed lives and hearts.

Sit quietly and think about the miracles that you saw this past week. Write them down and thank God for His hand in your life. Share the miracles with your child and explain how they are miracles. By recognizing miracles in everyday life, your child will learn about Jesus' hand in his life, just as the disciples did.

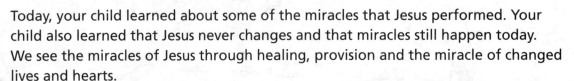

Activities for Home

1. Make a Miracle Chart. Every time a miracle happens within your family, write it down on the Miracle Chart.

2. Each night, have family prayer time and thank God for the miracles of that day.

3. Encourage your child to share a miracle he has experienced with a friend.

4. Jesus will work miracles for you. Read these stories in:
   John 2:1–11; Matthew 14:22–33, 17:24–27; John 21:1–13

✿ Let's Create ✿

── Items Needed ──

- One copy of the Fish Pattern (page 30) on construction paper for each child.

- Scissors and crayons or felt pens

- Large piece of netting in which to place paper fish (or create a net using the directions in the extension activity)

1. Instruct children to cut out copies of the Fish Pattern (page 30). Have precut Fish Patterns available for children who may have difficulty cutting.

2. Help children write or draw pictures on the fish of miracles they have experienced.

3. Let children put the fish in the miracle net you provide.

Extension Activity

── Items Needed ──

- 200 1" x 6" (2.5 cm x 15 cm) strips of paper. 200 strips will make a net approximately 4 feet square (1.2 m²).

- tape

1. Instruct children to make paper chains that are about 4' (1.2 m) long. Loop the chains together to make a net.

2. Let children place their miracle fish in the net. Hang the net from the ceiling.

✿ Let's Puzzle ✿

Photocopy the Many Miracles worksheet (page 31) for each child. Use in class or as a take-home sheet.

✿ Let's Review and Pray ✿

1. Review the miracles Jesus performed in today's lesson.

2. Ask children to look for miracles this week.

3. Say this prayer:

   Dear Father God, You have shown us Your love and power through the miracles of Your Son. Help us to see the many miracles in our lives. In the name of Your Son, Jesus Christ. Amen.

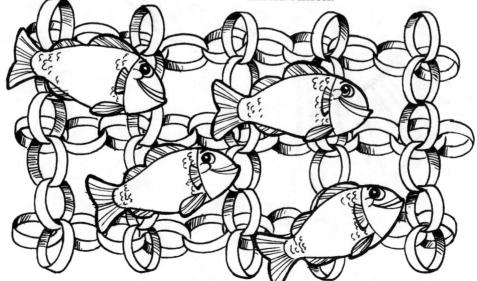

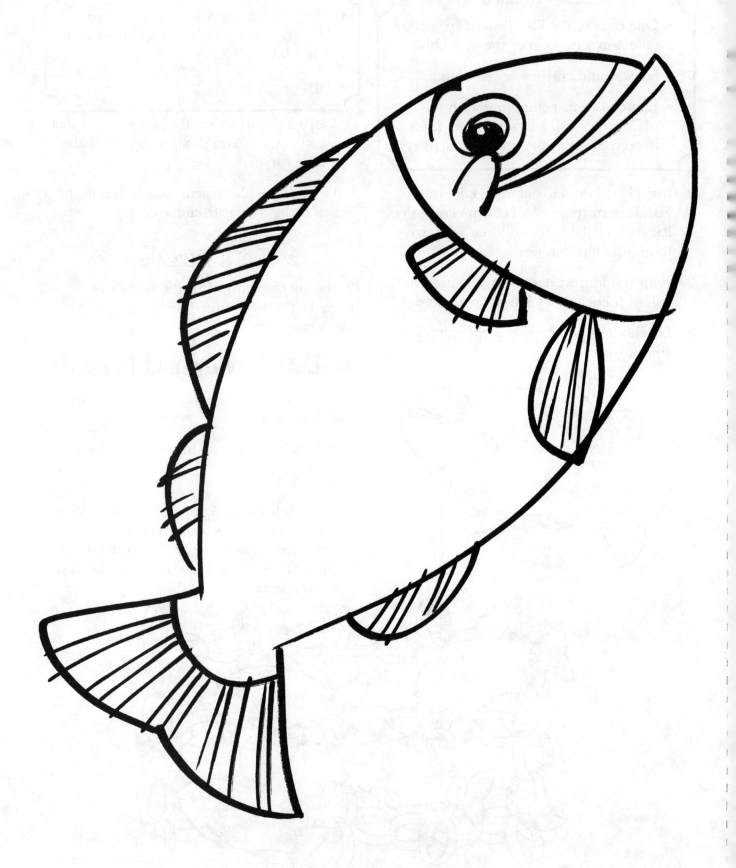

30

❧ Many Miracles ❧

Directions: Color the pictures of the miracles that Jesus performed.

*"People were overwhelmed with amazement. 'He has done everything well,'
they said. 'He even makes the deaf hear and the mute speak.'"*

Mark 7:37

Jesus Feeds the Hungry
❧ Prepare Your Heart ❧

Blessed are those who hunger and thirst for righteousness, for they will be filled. Matthew 5:6

Then Jesus declared, "I am the bread of life. He who comes to me will never go hungry, and he who believes in me will never be thirsty." John 6:35

We know that Jesus fed the hungry. He fed people both physical food and spiritual food. Since He is no longer here in body, He relies on His children to feed the hungry. As a parent or Sunday school teacher, you are preparing to "feed His lambs." Think about physical and spiritual ways that you can nurture those in your care. Just as Peter was commissioned by the Lord to "feed my lambs" (John 21:15), so are we entrusted with this responsibility.

Caution: Before completing any food activity, ask parent's permission and inquire about food allergies or other food preferences.

❧ Let's Begin ❧

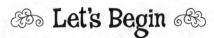

Items Needed

- Package of a food item for children (popcorn, fish-shaped crackers, fruit)

1. Say to the children, "Today, we are going to learn that Jesus fed His friends and that He fed the crowds. He gave everyone food." Ask for a helper to distribute the food.

2. Once the food is distributed, say a blessing, thanking Jesus for providing it.

❧ Let's Listen ❧

1. Photocopy and cut the *Jesus Feeds the Hungry* mini-book (pages 33–37) so that you have a set for each child in the class and an extra set for a sample book.

2. Read the *Jesus Feeds the Hungry* mini-book to the class.

3. Distribute a mini-book to each child. While children are coloring the pages, engage them with the following questions:

- Why did Jesus feed the crowds?

- Why did He feed His friends?

- Tell the class about a time when you invited a friend to eat with you.

- In what ways can we feed people who are physically hungry? (gifts of food or meals, food drives, shelters)

- In what ways can we feed people who are spiritually hungry? (pray for them, encourage them with love and kindness, tell them about Jesus)

JESUS FEEDS THE HUNGRY

CD-204054 • *Jesus Saves! Take-Home Mini-Books*

"Master, the people are getting hungry," a disciple said to Jesus. "There's no food."
"I have five loaves of bread," said one boy, "and I have two fish."
Jesus broke the bread and fish into pieces. "Feed the people," Jesus said.
Five thousand people ate.

Jesus fed the crowd. Jesus feeds you.

A large crowd gathered on the mountainside.
Jesus said, "These people have been with me for days and have had nothing to eat."
Jesus took seven loaves of bread, thanked God, divided them, and gave four
thousand people food. There were seven baskets of food left over.

Jesus fed the people. Jesus feeds you.

The disciples met in the upper room for the Passover Feast. Jesus took the bread, broke it, and said, "Take and eat. This is my body given for you."
Jesus took the cup, and the disciples drank from it. Jesus said, "This is my blood, poured out for many."

Jesus fed the disciples. Jesus feeds you.

One morning, the disciples caught many fish. Jesus said to them, "Bring me some of the fish you have just caught."
The disciples hurried to shore where Jesus sat by the fire. He said, "Come, have breakfast." He gave them bread and fish.

Jesus fed His friends. Jesus feeds you. **8**

❧ Note to Parents ❧

Today, your child learned that Jesus fed the hungry. He fed the crowds, and He fed His friends. He fed them both physically and spiritually.

Think about some spiritual and physical ways that you and your family can follow Jesus' example and feed others.

Activities for Home

1. Think of ways to spiritually feed others, such as an encouraging word, a smile, an offer of forgiveness, or other acts of kindness.

2. Think of ways to physically feed others. Help your child take food to a homeless shelter, invite friends over for dinner, or take food to an elderly neighbor.

3. Let your child say the blessing before each meal this week.

4. Jesus feeds you. Read these stories in:
   John 6:1–15; Matthew 15:32–38, 26:17–29; John 21:1–14

❧ Let's Create ❧
─ Items Needed ─

- Fish Patterns (page 39)

- Pieces of foam board or construction paper

- Scissors, glue, crayons or felt pens

- Old compact discs (two per child)

- Two craft eyes per child if using foam board (Use eye patterns on page 39 if using construction paper.)

- Ribbon or fishing line

1. Prepare a sample fish CD. If using craft foam, use the Fish Patterns (page 39) as templates. Or, copy the pattern pieces on construction paper.

2. Help children decorate and cut out the fish patterns. Have precut patterns available for children who may have difficulty cutting.

3. Instruct children to glue the tails and fins on the non-shiny sides of the compact discs. Glue the two discs together—shiny sides facing out. Have them glue the craft (or paper) eyes on either sides of the discs. Fold the center fin and place it though the center hole of the discs.

4. To hang the fish, glue ribbon or fishing line to the tops of the discs.

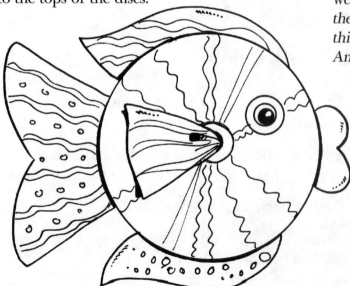

Extension Activity
─ Items Needed ─

- Fishing stick or pole with a magnet in place of a hook

- Box of large, metal paper clips (Butterfly clips work well.)

- String, ribbon, or fishing line

When children have finished their fish, attach a large paper clip to the mouth of each fish. Have children sit in a circle. Spread the fish out in the middle of the circle. Pass the stick or pole with the magnet attached around the circle and let children take turns trying to catch their own fish.

❧ Let's Puzzle ❧

Photocopy the Feed the Hungry worksheet (page 40) for each child. Use in class or as a take-home sheet.

❧ Let's Review and Pray ❧

1. Discuss ways that we can be like Jesus and meet the physical and spiritual needs of others.

3. Say this prayer:

Dear Father God, thank You for the food we have to eat. You have asked us to feed the hungry. Please help us find ways to do this. In the name of Your Son, Jesus Christ. Amen.

🌸 Fish Patterns 🌸

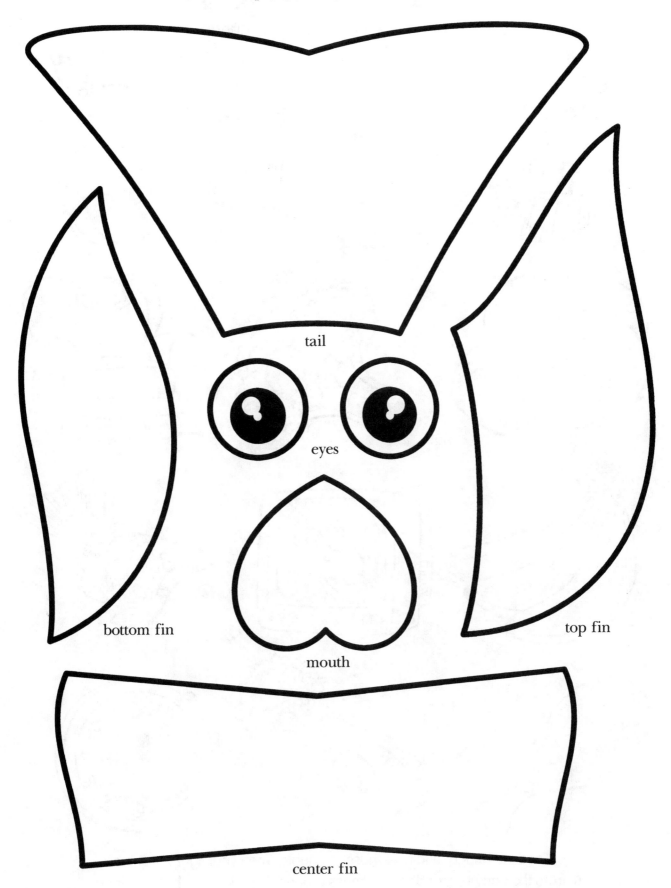

tail

eyes

bottom fin

top fin

mouth

center fin

Jesus Saves! Take-Home Mini-Books • CD-204054

Feed the Hungry

Directions: Circle the items that you could feed to the hungry.

"Feed the hungry and help those in trouble. Then your light will shine
out from the darkness, and the darkness around you will be as bright as noon."

Isaiah 58:10 NLT

Jesus Heals
ꙮ Prepare Your Heart ꙮ

Praise the LORD, O my soul; all my inmost being, praise his holy name. Praise the LORD, O my soul, and forget not all his benefits—who forgives all your sins and heals all your diseases, who redeems your life from the pit and crowns you with love and compassion, who satisfies your desires with good things so that your youth is renewed like the eagle's. Psalm 103:1–5

Pay special attention to the passage, "who forgives all your sins and heals all your diseases." (Psalm 103:3) Do you notice the word *all*? God's promise is to forgive *all* your sins and heal *all* your diseases. He does this through His Son, Jesus Christ. As a believer in Christ, you can trust God's Word and stand on His promise. In the stories of this lesson, people who were healed had faith that they would be healed.

Jesus healed every person who came to Him for healing. He healed with a touch, with spoken words, and with the faith of the believer. He healed the sick, the injured, and delivered those filled with demons. The act of healing is one of the ways that Jesus shows us His power and His love. Because Jesus "is the same yesterday and today and forever" (Hebrews 13:8), we can believe Him for the healing of our spirits and bodies.

ꙮ Let's Begin ꙮ

⎯ Items Needed ⎯

- A paper bag

- First aid supplies, such as adhesive bandages, an empty pill bottle, cotton balls, etc.

- Other generic items, such as a picture of praying hands, a toothbrush, crayons, a rock, a doll, etc.

1. Pass around the bag of items and instruct each child to pick out one item. Then, go around the class and ask each child to explain whether his item can be used to heal.

2. Tell children that Jesus has healed many different people. Jesus has the power to heal with a touch, His words, and with our faith.

ꙮ Let's Listen ꙮ

1. Photocopy and cut the *Jesus Heals* mini-book (pages 42–46) so that you have a set for each child in the class and an extra set for a sample book.

2. Read the *Jesus Heals* mini-book to the class.

3. Distribute a mini-book to each child. While children are coloring the pages, engage them with the following questions:

- In what ways does Jesus heal the people in these stories?

- Jesus healed the blind. Put your hands over your eyes. How does it feel now that you cannot see?

- Jesus healed the paralyzed. What would you do if you could not walk?

JESUS HEALS

CD-204054 • *Jesus Saves! Take-Home Mini-Books*

"My daughter! My daughter!" the official said as he knelt before Jesus. "She is only 12 years old, and she is dying."
Jesus said, "Don't be afraid. Just believe."

Jesus said, "I will heal your little girl." And He did.

Two blind men sat by the road. Jesus walked by. The blind men jumped up and called to Jesus, "Son of David, have mercy on us. We want to see."

Jesus said, "I will heal you." And He did.

The water stirred in the pool. People jumped in to be healed.
"Help me," a lame man cried. "I can't walk to the pool."

Jesus said, "I will heal the man." And He did.

A father ran to Jesus. "Bad spirits are making my son very sick."
The disciples said, "We cannot heal him."
Jesus pointed to the child. "Leave the boy alone." The evil spirits went away.

Jesus said, "I will heal the boy." And He did.

8

Note to Parents

Jesus heals many people. He heals the sick, the injured, and delivers those filled with demons. Jesus wants us to call on Him when we are sick, injured, or troubled.

In today's lesson, your child learned that Jesus heals by word, touch, and the believer's faith. Talk to your child about times when your family members have been healed. Talk to your child about the role that prayer and faith had in the healing.

Activities for Home

1. Bake cookies with your child. Deliver them to someone who needs healing.

2. Has your child ever been sick or injured? Have him write a thank-you note to Jesus for healing him.

3. Let your child choose one of the stories from the mini-book. Ask her to pretend that she is the person asking Jesus for help. Encourage your child to always thank Jesus for His help.

4. Jesus healed you. Read these stories in:
   1 Peter 2:24; Mark 5:22–24, 35–43; Matthew 20:29–34; John 5:1–9; Matthew 17:14–18

🍃 Let's Create 🍃

⎯ Items Needed ⎯

- Copies of the Lame Man Puppet Patterns (page 48)

- Two sturdy 9" (22.9 cm) round dinner-sized paper plates for each child

- Crayons, markers, or colorful pencils

- Rulers

- Scissors and white glue that dries clear

- Brass paper fasteners

- Craft sticks

1. Prepare a sample Lame Man puppet.

2. Have children color and cut out the Lame Man Puppet Patterns (page 48). Have precut patterns available for children who may have difficulty cutting.

3. Glue the head, body, and feet on the paper plate and cut out the figures.

4. Glue the head and body together.

5. Attach the feet to the body with the fastener.

6. Make the lame man's bed by cutting a 2" x 5" (5.1 cm x 12.7 cm) piece from the paper plate. Using the dashed lines, cut a slit on both sides of the arm and slip the bed through the slits.

7. Glue the craft stick onto the back of the body for a handle (see figure below). When dry, push on the handle and watch the once lame man walk after being healed by Jesus.

Extension Activity

Select a child to pretend to be Jesus. Have children approach the pretend Jesus with their Lame Man Puppets to be healed. After all of the puppets have been healed, have children march around the room with their puppets, singing "Onward Christian Soldiers."

🍃 Let's Puzzle 🍃

Photocopy the Jesus Heals worksheet (page 49) for each child. Use in class or as a takehome sheet.

🍃 Let's Review and Pray 🍃

1. Remind children of what they can do if they are sick: pray, believe in God's promise to heal, and ask others to pray and believe with them.

2. Review the ways that Jesus heals.

3. Say this prayer:

   Dear Father God, thank you for Your promise to heal us of all our diseases. We love You. In the name of Your Son, Jesus Christ, Amen.

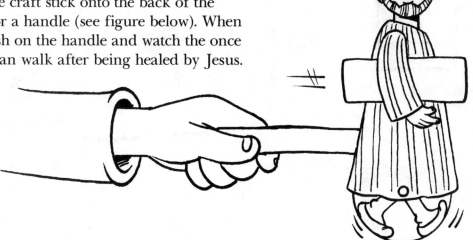

❦ Lame Man Puppet Patterns ❦

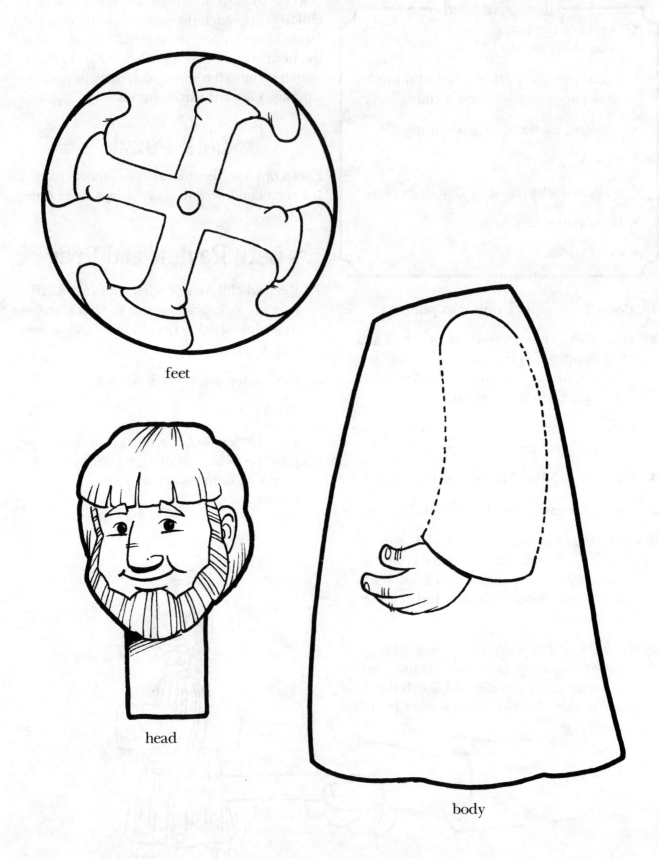

feet

head

body

✇ Jesus Heals ✇

Directions: What diseases does the Lord promise to heal?
Find the answer in Psalm 103:2–3 and hidden in the picture below.

Write the word on the lines. ___ ___ ___

"Praise the Lord, O my soul . . . who forgives all your sins and heals all your diseases. . . . "
Psalm 103:2–3

Jesus Forgives
❧ Prepare Your Heart ❧

Therefore, as God's chosen people, holy and dearly loved, clothe yourselves with compassion, kindness, humility, gentleness and patience. Bear with each other and forgive whatever grievances you may have against one another. Forgive as the Lord forgave you. And over all these virtues put on love, which binds them all together in perfect unity. Colossians 3:12–14

If we confess our sins, he is faithful and just and will forgive us our sins and purify us from all unrighteousness. 1 John 1:9

Jesus died so that our sins would be forgiven. We are forgiven when we ask God for forgiveness and believe in Jesus, the Son of God. As children of God, we must also forgive each other.

Sit quietly in prayer and make a list of your sins. Hand them over to God and accept His forgiveness. When you have done this, you will be ready to help children do the same. Remember, God forgives because of His great and perfect love for us.

❧ Let's Begin ❧

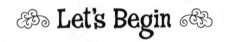

── Items Needed ──

- Sheet of paper and pencil
- Bible

1. Discuss Jesus' promise to forgive our sins. Ask the children, "What are sins? What things do you need to ask Jesus to forgive you for?"

2. On the sheet of paper, list the examples children offer. You might need to suggest other areas of sin, such as telling lies, hitting someone, or not doing chores.

3. Fold the list and place it in the Bible. Explain that when we confess our sins to Jesus, He always forgives us.

❧ Let's Listen ❧

1. Photocopy and cut the *Jesus Forgives* mini-book (pages 51–55) so that you have a set for each child in the class and an extra set for a sample book.

2. Read the *Jesus Forgives* mini-book to the class.

3. Distribute a mini-book to each child. While children are coloring the pages, engage them with the following questions:

- Can you tell me about a time when you forgave someone? What happened after you forgave?

- What were some of things that Jesus did to show that He forgave the people in the stories?

- What are some ways that you can show your forgiveness?

JESUS FORGIVES

CD-204054 • *Jesus Saves! Take-Home Mini-Books*

"Hey, he hit me!"
Jesus said, "Don't hit him back. Turn the other cheek."
"I don't like him."
Jesus said, "Don't fight him. Love your enemies and pray for them."

Jesus forgave His enemies. Jesus always forgives you.

"Lord, this woman has been very bad. We must stone her!"
Jesus said, "If any of you have never been bad, go ahead and throw your rock."
The men, one by one, dropped their rocks and walked away.
Jesus said to the woman, "Go and change your life."

Jesus forgave the woman. Jesus always forgives you.

A tax collector climbed a tree to see Jesus.
Jesus looked up. "Zacchaeus, I want to stay at your house today."
The people muttered, "Don't stay with him. He's a sinner."
Zacchaeus said, "I will change and do good things."

Jesus forgave Zacchaeus. Jesus always forgives you.

Soldiers came to arrest Jesus.
"Don't touch Him!" a disciple shouted to the soldiers. Simon Peter drew his sword.
He cut off one soldier's ear.
Jesus said, "Put back your sword." He touched the soldier's ear and healed it.

Jesus forgave the soldier. Jesus always forgives you.

🌸 Note to Parents 🌸

Today, you child learned that Jesus forgives sins. Likewise, as children of God, we must forgive others.

Sit quietly in prayer and make a list of your sins. Hand them over to God and accept His forgiveness. When you have done this, you will be ready to help your child do the same. Remember, because of God's great love for us, He sent Jesus to pay the price for our sins.

🌸 🌸 🌸 🌸 🌸 🌸

Activities for Home

1. Help your child discuss one of her sins. Write this sin on a piece of paper. Help her pray for forgiveness. Then, take the word or list and tuck it into the Bible— visually giving the list to God. Later in the week, take out the list and go over any results of this activity with your child.

2. Encourage your child to show forgiveness to someone whom he needs to forgive. Your child could make a card for or call the person he needs to forgive. If the person is a friend, plan a special play date or an invitation to dinner.

3. Jesus always forgives you. Read these stories in:
    Matthew 5:38–44; John 8:1–11; Luke 19:1–10, 22:47–51

🌸 Let's Create 🌸

⎯ Items Needed ⎯

- One copy of the Paper Rock Pattern (page 57) on brown or gray construction paper for each child. (You may choose to use real rocks instead.)

- Scissors, glue, tape, magazine pictures, tempera paints, and crayons or felt pens

1. Prepare a sample rock.

2. Give each child a rock or use the Paper Rock Pattern (page 57). Have children cut on the solid lines and fold on the dotted lines. Have precut rock patterns available for children who may have difficulty cutting. Tape together.

3. Have each child paint, draw, or cut from magazines examples of positive things that we can do or say toward others. Remind children that instead of throwing stones to hurt, we can do and say positive things that bring healing and joy to others.

   * To save time, cut out pictures in advance for children.

Extension Activity

⎯ Item Needed ⎯

- Chalk or a hopscotch board

With chalk, draw a hopscotch game on the sidewalk, or use a hopscotch board in the classroom. Write positive words in each square. Teach children how to play hopscotch using their stones as markers.

🌸 Let's Puzzle 🌸

Photocopy the Friends Forgive worksheet (page 58 for each child. Use in class or as a take-home sheet.

🌸 Let's Review and Pray 🌸

1. Review Jesus' faithfulness to forgive us of our sins. Discuss ways that we can show forgiveness to others.

2. Say this prayer:

   Dear Father God, thank you for forgiving our sins. You have asked us to forgive our enemies. Help us to forgive so that we may be forgiven. In the name of Your Son, Jesus Christ. Amen.

❧ Paper Rock Pattern ❧

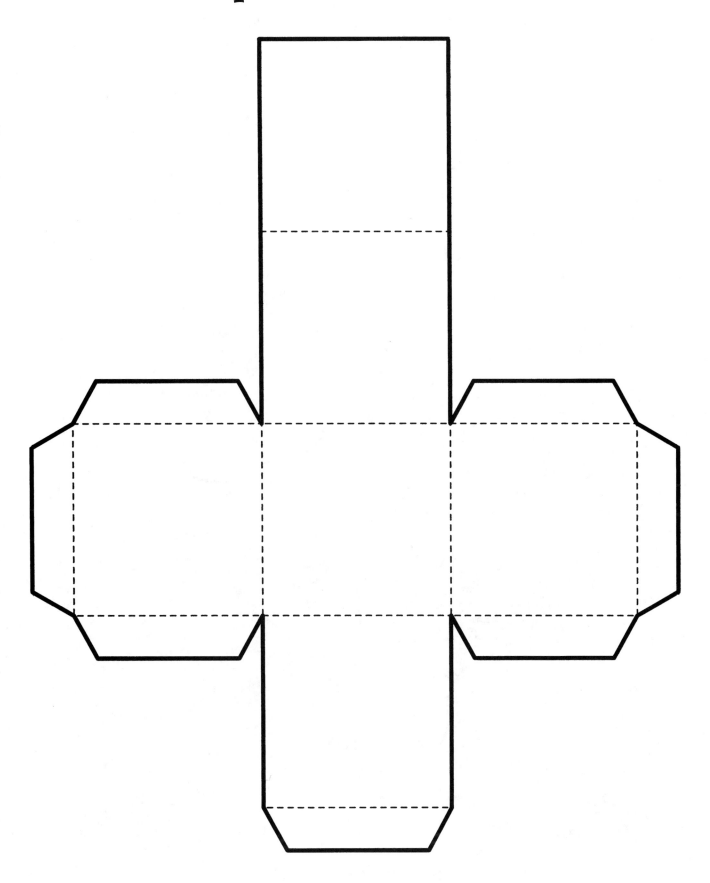

© Carson-Dellosa

57

Jesus Saves! Take-Home Mini-Books • CD-204054

❧ Friends Forgive ❧

Directions: Mario wants to forgive his friend for calling him a bad name. Follow the maze to help Mario find his friend playing in the sandbox.

START

FINISH

"Forgive as the Lord forgave you."
Colossians 3:13

Jesus Brings Joy
Prepare Your Heart

Rejoice in the Lord always. . . . Do not be anxious about anything, but in everything, by prayer and petition, with thanksgiving, present your requests to God. And the peace of God, which transcends all understanding, will guard your hearts and your minds in Christ Jesus. . . . whatever is true, whatever is noble, whatever is right, whatever is pure, whatever is lovely, whatever is admirable—if anything is excellent or praiseworthy—think about such things. Whatever you have learned or received or heard from me, or seen in me—put it into practice. And the God of peace will be with you. Philippians 4:4–9

Some people think that if they acquire material things, they will be happy. Joy that comes from material things is only temporary. True and eternal joy comes from having a relationship with the Lord. Jesus said that if you obey His commands and stay in His love, you will be filled with His joy. (John 15:10–12) Therefore, it is important to follow God's Word and meditate on His love. This will bring us the joy that Jesus wants us to have.

Today's lesson shows several instances in which Jesus brought joy to those around Him. Jesus brings deep, long-lasting joy to our lives when we have a close relationship with Him.

Let's Begin

1. With children sitting in a circle, tell them to make mad faces. They should make them as mean and ugly as they can.

2. Then, instruct them to make happy faces. Tell them to smile and laugh.

3. Ask them which face felt better.

4. Tell them that it takes more muscles to frown than it does to smile and ask which is going to be easier to do.

Let's Listen

1. Photocopy and cut the *Jesus Brings Joy* mini-book (pages 60–64) so that you have a set for each child in the class and an extra set for a sample book.

2. Read the *Jesus Brings Joy* mini-book to the class.

3. Distribute a mini-book to each child. While children are coloring the pages, engage them with the following questions:

   • Joy comes from having Jesus in your heart and from knowing that He loves you and is with you all the time. Because you have a relationship with Jesus, you can feel joy even when you are having a bad day. What are some examples of joy in your life?

   • What brings you joy?

   • What do you do with your family that brings you joy?

   • Who brings you joy?

JESUS BRINGS JOY

CD-204054 • *Jesus Saves! Take-Home Mini-Books*

Many people came to hear Jesus. His disciples sat around Him. Jesus said, "Blessed are you who weep now, for you will laugh. Rejoice in that day and leap for joy, because great is your reward in heaven." The people smiled.

Jesus brought joy to the crowd. Jesus brings joy to you.

2

Jesus' friend Lazarus was very sick, and he died. He was buried in a cave.
Lazarus's sisters, Mary and Martha, cried.
Jesus said, "Do not be sad. Your brother will rise again."
Then, Jesus spoke to Lazarus, "Lazarus, come out!"
Lazarus walked out of the cave.

3

Jesus brought joy to His friends. Jesus brings joy to you.

Jesus' face shone like the sun. His clothes sparkled like white light. Moses and Elijah appeared. They talked with Jesus.
God spoke from a cloud, "This is My Son. I love Him. Listen to Him."

Jesus brought joy to His Father. Jesus brings joy to you.

6

"Peace be with you," Jesus said.
The disciples saw that Jesus was alive, but Thomas did not believe. Jesus let Thomas touch the scars in His hands and side.
Thomas said, "I believe."

Jesus brought joy to the disciples. Jesus brings joy to you. **8**

✿ Note to Parents ✿

Today, the class discussed the joy that comes from knowing Jesus. Your child learned that true joy comes from having a relationship with the Lord.

Today's lesson shows several examples of Jesus bringing joy to those around Him through close fellowship with Him. Help your child understand that Jesus brings joy to our lives every day when we live in fellowship with Him. Explain that we fellowship with Jesus by reading the Bible, praying, and focusing our attention on God by talking to Him throughout the day.

Activities for Home

1. Gather your family and encourage each one to say something he especially likes about each member of the family. Watch the joyous smiles form on their faces.

2. Encourage your child to bring joy to others by drawing a picture for someone he loves and sending it to him.

3. Jesus brings joy to you. Read these stories in:
   Matthew 5:1–11; John 11:1–44; Matthew 17:1–13; John 20:19–31

9

❧ Let's Create ❧

⸻ Items Needed ⸻

- One copy of the Joy Mobile Patterns (page 66) on white or colorful construction paper for each child

- Scissors, glue, and crayons or felt pens

- Single hole-punch

- Large paper clips (one per child)

- Fishing line, ribbon, or yarn

1. Prepare a sample Joy Mobile.

2. Distribute copies of the Joy Mobile Patterns (page 66) to children. Use white paper if you want children to color the letters; use colorful copies to save time.

3. Instruct children to cut out the letters. Have precut letters available for children who may have difficulty cutting. Hole-punch the letters where indicated.

4. Using the letters and fishing line, guide children to make a mobile of the word *JOY* by attaching the *O* to the bottom of the *J* and the *Y* to the bottom of the *O*. Bend a paper clip into an *S* shape and use it as the hook for the top. Hang the mobiles in the classroom or let children take them home to hang in their rooms.

Extension Activity

⸻ Items Needed ⸻

- Collection of pictures that show happy situations—either cut out of magazines or drawn by children

Create a bulletin board titled, "Happiness In the Lord." Have children select or draw pictures to attach to the display.

❧ Let's Puzzle ❧

Photocopy the Jesus Brings Joy worksheet (page 67) for each child. Use in class or as a take-home sheet.

❧ Let's Review and Pray ❧

1. Remind the class what Jesus did to bring joy to His family and friends.

2. Ask how children can share this joy with others. For example: smile at someone, tell someone, "I love you," or hug someone.

3. Say this prayer:

Dear Father God, we are filled with joy knowing how much You love us. Help us to keep our thoughts on Your love so that we can always feel and share this joy. In the name of Your Son, Jesus Christ. Amen.

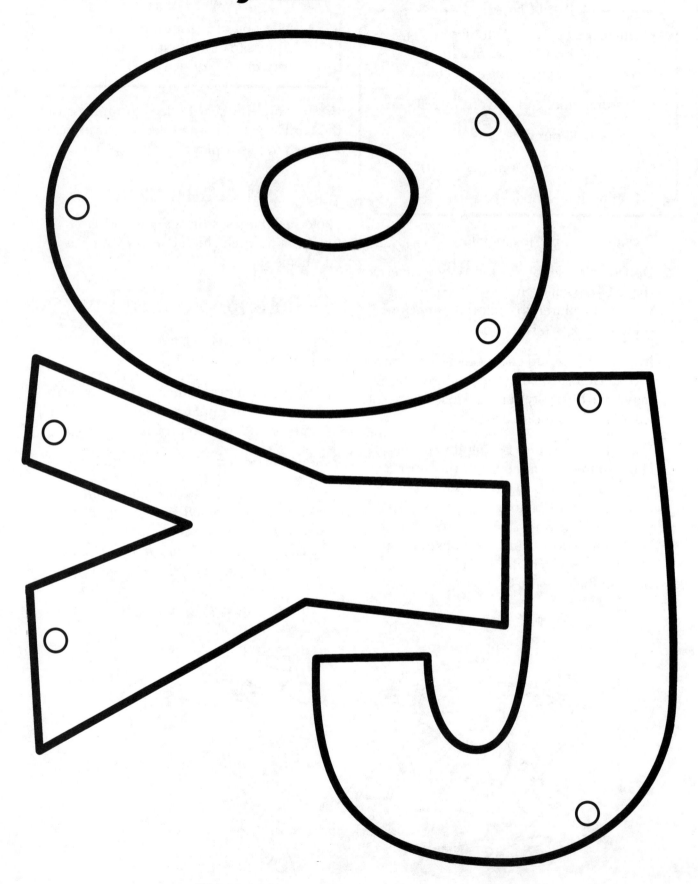

Jesus Brings Joy

Directions: Fit the words in the correct spaces to complete the crossword below. One letter has been placed for you.

HAPPY   JESUS   JOY   LOVE   PEACE   SMILE

"Do not grieve, for the joy of the Lord is your strength."
Nehemiah 8:10

Jesus Saves! Take-Home Mini-Books • CD-204054

Jesus Renews
❧ Prepare Your Heart ❧

I sought the LORD, and he answered me; he delivered me from all my fears. Those who look to him are radiant; their faces are never covered with shame. . . . The angel of the LORD encamps around those who fear him, and he delivers them. . . . The righteous cry out, and the LORD hears them; he delivers them from all their troubles. The LORD is close to the brokenhearted and saves those who are crushed in spirit. A righteous man may have many troubles, but the LORD delivers him from them all. . . . Psalm 34:4–19

. . . but those who hope in the LORD will renew their strength. They will soar on wings like eagles; they will run and not grow weary, they will walk and not be faint. Isaiah 40:31

Our emotions are often a barometer that indicates how much we are letting God renew our spirit. There will always be circumstances and challenges. Do we trust God to see us through? Do we sit with Him and let Him lift our spirits on the wings of eagles? Sit quietly and think of the circumstances in your life that are causing you stress. Mentally hand them over to Jesus. When tempted to worry again, remind yourself that you gave these burdens to Jesus.

❧ Let's Begin ❧

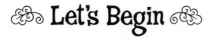

── Item Needed ──
- Cross (plaque, picture, or other)

1. If a cross is not already in the room, bring one in and hang it on the wall or set it on a stand.

2. Have children sit around the cross. Share one of your problems with the children. Write it on a piece of paper and show children that you are putting it at the foot of the cross.

3. Ask children to share something that is bothering or upsetting them. Write the problem on a piece of paper. Let them put the paper at the foot of the cross. Explain that they are giving the problem to Jesus.

❧ Let's Listen ❧

1. Photocopy and cut the *Jesus Renews* mini-book (pages 69–73) so that you have a set for each child in the class and an extra set for a sample book.

2. Read the *Jesus Renews* mini-book to the class.

3. Distribute a mini-book to each child. While children are coloring the pages, engage them with the following questions:

- How did Jesus renew the people in the stories?

- Who likes to take naps? Can you pray to Jesus during rest times? Ask children to share some of the things for which they can pray.

- Can you be like Jesus and help renew a friend or family member? What are some ways that you can do this? (help a brother or sister with chores, play with a little brother or sister, speak kindly to family members and friends)

JESUS RENEWS

Jesus saw a man with a shriveled hand and said, "Hold out your hand."
The man lifted his hand. Jesus healed it.

Jesus renewed the man's hand. Jesus renews you.

A woman who had been bleeding for many years crawled through the crowd. She said, "If only I could touch his cloak, I would be better." She touched Jesus' cloak. Jesus turned to her and said, "Daughter, your faith has healed you. Go in peace."

Jesus renewed the woman. Jesus renews you.

Some tired and sad children walked into town.
Jesus said, "Come to Me, all of you who are weary and burdened. I am gentle and humble in heart, and you will find rest for your souls with me."
The children smiled at Jesus.

Jesus renewed the children. Jesus renews you.

Jesus' friend Mary poured expensive perfume on His feet and head. A disciple complained, "Lord, we could sell that perfume."
Jesus smiled. "Her many sins have been forgiven because she showed her love for Me."

Jesus renewed Mary. Jesus renews you.

Note to Parents

Today, your child learned that God renews our strength when we have difficult circumstances. Your child also learned ways that he can give his problems to Jesus.

In Psalm 34:17–22 and Isaiah 40:31, the Lord promises to renew our strength if we abide in Him. Sit quietly and think of the circumstances in your life that are causing you stress. Mentally hand them over to Jesus.

Activities for Home

1. With your child, list some of the problems your family is facing. Explain to him that you are trusting God to keep you strong and faithful through the difficulty.

2. Discuss with your child any problems she is facing. Help her write each problem on a piece of paper. Tuck them in her Bible and together turn them over to God.

3. As a family, schedule a time to sit and share quiet time with the Lord. Meditating on the Lord is a good habit for your child to develop.

4. Jesus renews you. Read these stories in:
   Matthew 12:9–13, 9:20–22, 11:25–30; Luke 7:36–50

❧ Let's Create ❧

— Items Needed —

- One copy of the Rainbow Pattern (page 75) for each child.
- Scissors, glue, crayons or felt pens, card stock, single hole-punch, string
- Three copies of the Cloud Pattern (below) for each child

1. Using card stock, make three copies of the Cloud Pattern (below) for each child.

2. Distribute three copies of the Cloud Pattern to each child. Instruct children to draw a picture on each cloud or write about something that makes them tired or sad.

3. Distribute the Rainbow Pattern (page 75). Let children color their rainbows. Explain that the rainbow is a reminder that God keeps all of His promises.

4. Using a single hole-punch and string, have children attach their clouds under the rainbow. Explain how they can give their sad feelings to God.

Extension Activity

— Items Needed —

- A large, hand-drawn cloud made from white paper.
- Strips of multi-colorful crepe paper

Make a rainbow mobile. Help children staple strips of colorful crepe paper to the ends of the large cloud. Hang the cloud from the ceiling.

Form a circle beneath the rainbow and lead children in reciting Isaiah 40:31 and Psalm 103:5.

❧ Let's Puzzle ❧

Photocopy the He Gives Me Strength worksheet (page 76) for each child. Use in class or as a take-home sheet.

❧ Let's Review and Pray ❧

1. Review why it is important to sit quietly and pray to God. (As we spend time with Him, he renews us and gives us strength.)

2. Say this prayer:

   Dear Father God, You have promised to renew our strength. Help us to receive this blessing from You. Thank you. In the name of your Son, Jesus Christ. Amen.

3. Have everyone close his eyes and have a quiet time with Jesus.

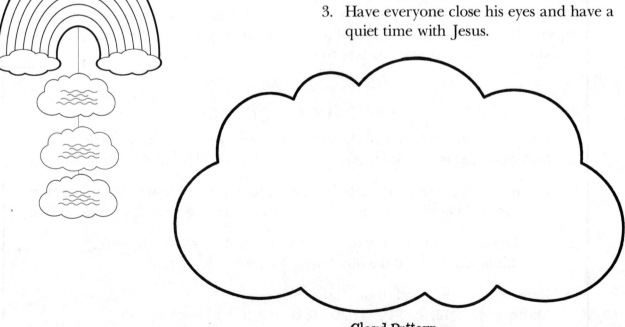

Cloud Pattern

❧ Rainbow Pattern ❧

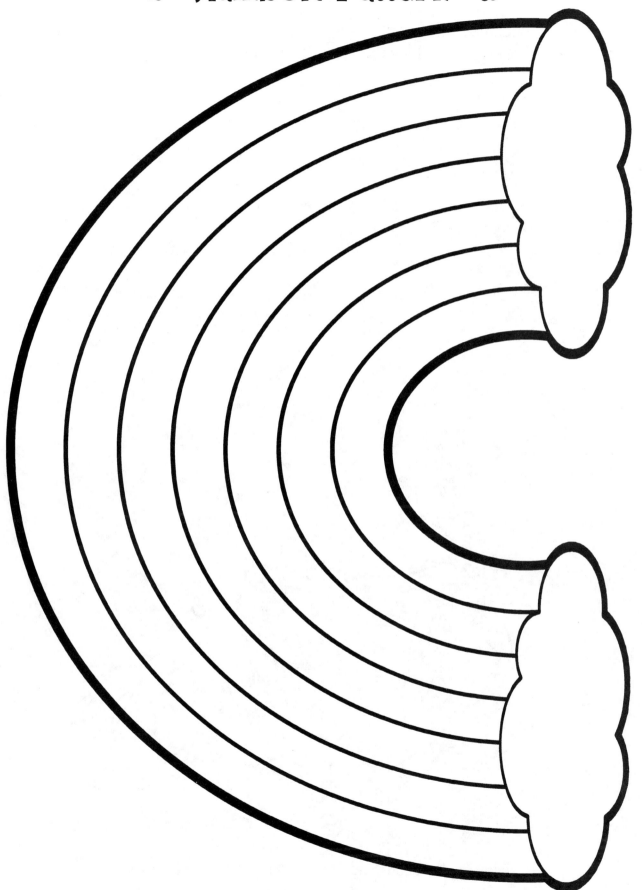

75

He Gives Me Strength

Directions: Connect the dots. Use the picture and the verse below to complete the following sentence. God makes me strong like an _____.

"He fills my life with good things. My youth is renewed like the eagle's!"
Psalm 103:5 NLT

Jesus Prays
❧ Prepare Your Heart ❧

"Again, I tell you that if two of you on earth agree about anything you ask for, it will be done for you by my Father in heaven. For where two or three come together in my name, there am I with them." Matthew 18:19–20

Whenever you pray, Jesus is there with you. What an astounding truth! God honored the prayers of His Son, Jesus. God honors the prayers of children. He honors your prayers, as well. Ask the Lord to bless your time with the children. He will!

In the following lesson, children will learn that Jesus prayed many times to His Father. They, too, can pray anytime and anywhere, and God will listen to them as He listened to His Son.

❧ Let's Begin ❧

Instruct children to stand in a circle holding hands. Explain that you are going to say a prayer that Jesus taught His disciples, called the Lord's Prayer. (Matthew 6:9–13) Jesus wants us to know the prayer, also. If children do not know the prayer, say one line at a time and have them repeat after you.

❧ Let's Listen ❧

1. Photocopy and cut the *Jesus Prays* mini-book (pages 78–82) so that you have a set for each child in the class and an extra set for a sample book.

2. Read the *Jesus Prays* mini-book to the class.

3. Distribute a mini-book to each child. While children are coloring the pages, engage them with the following questions:

   - Why did Jesus go to a special place to pray? Name some of the places where He prayed.

   - We pray in church. Is this the only place God listens to our prayers? Name some of the other places where you can pray. (List the places children have prayed.)

   - Why did you pray in each of these places? (List the reason for prayer next to each location.) Point out that God listened to and honored every prayer.

JESUS PRAYS

The disciples wanted Jesus to teach them how to pray.
Jesus said to them, "When you pray, say, Father, hallowed be Your name, Your kingdom come. Give us each day our daily bread. Forgive us our sins, for we also forgive everyone who sins against us. And lead us not into temptation."

7

God the Father listened to Jesus. God the Father listens to you. **2**

One day, Jesus talked to over 5,000 people. He was very tired. Jesus needed to rest. He needed to pray. Jesus climbed a mountain to pray alone. **3**

God the Father listened to Jesus. God the Father listens to you.

4

Jesus went with His disciples to a grove of trees. Jesus said, "Sit here while I go over there and pray."
The disciples fell asleep. Jesus went by himself and prayed to God.

5

God the Father listened to Jesus. God the Father listens to you.   **6**

Jesus had dinner with His disciples and friends. After dinner, He prayed for Himself. Then, He prayed for the disciples. After He prayed for the disciples, He prayed for all believers. Jesus prayed for you.   **7**

God the Father listened to Jesus. God the Father listens to you. **8**

❧ Note to Parents ❧

In Matthew 18:19–20, Jesus says, "Again, I tell you that if two of you on earth agree about anything you ask for, it will be done for you by my Father in heaven. For where two or three come together in my name, there am I with them."

When you pray with your child, Jesus is there with you. God honored the prayers of His Son, Jesus. God honors the prayers of your children and your prayers as a family.

In today's lesson, your child learned that Jesus prayed many times to His Father, God. Your child also learned that he can pray anytime, anywhere, for any reason, and that God is listening.

Activities for Home

1. Instruct your child to decorate a prayer box and write the name of each person he loves on a piece of paper. He should put the names in the box. Each day, have him take out a name and pray for that person.

2. For a week, keep a list of all of the places where you and your child prayed.

3. Set aside a time for your family to pray together.

4. God the Father listens to you. Read these stories in:
   Luke 11:1–4; Matthew 14:22–23, 26:36–44; John 17:1–26.

✍️ Let's Create ✍️

Items Needed

- Two copies of the Cross Pattern (page 84) for each child
- Scissors and glue sticks
- Strips of colorful tissue paper
- Single hole-punch
- Yarn or ribbon

1. Prepare a sample stained-glass cross.

2. Distribute two copies of the Cross Pattern (page 84) to each child. Direct children to cut out the crosses from the middle of the black ovals of both patterns. Have precut cross patterns available for children who may have difficulty cutting the pattern.

3. Distribute strips of colorful tissue paper to each child. Instruct each child to glue the colorful tissue paper onto the back of the black oval—completely covering the area where the cross was.

4. Instruct each child to glue the other black oval over the tissue paper so that the stained glass craft will be double-sided. Be sure that children match the crosses so that the light shines through the "stained glass."

5. Punch out a circle at the top of the craft. Tie ribbon or yarn to the top. Encourage each child to hang his cross in a special prayer place.

Extension Activity

Stand in a circle and start a prayer of praise. Let each child take a turn thanking God for something in his life.

✍️ Let's Puzzle ✍️

Photocopy the Talking to God worksheet (page 85) for each child. Use in class or as a take-home sheet.

✍️ Let's Review and Pray ✍️

1. Review the list of places to pray and why we pray.

2. Remind children that they can pray anytime and anywhere and that God will hear them.

3. Say this prayer:

   Dear Father God, thank you for giving us the Lord's Prayer. Thank You for always hearing us—when we pray the Lord's Prayer or when we say our own words. In the name of Your Son, Jesus Christ. Amen.

❧ Cross Pattern ❧

84

❧ Talking to God ❧

Directions: Color each place where you can pray.

"Keep on praying."
1 Thessalonians 5:17 NLT

Jesus Saves! Take-Home Mini-Books • CD-204054

Jesus Loves You
✿ Prepare Your Heart ✿

For I am convinced that neither death nor life . . . nor anything else in all creation, will be able to separate us from the love of God that is in Christ Jesus our Lord. Romans 8:38–39

Close your eyes and think about how much God loves you. Write down the ways you have seen His love in the past week, month, or year. Be prepared to share some of those ways with your class. It is important to teach children that Jesus will always love them. He loves them even if it doesn't seem like anyone else loves them. Jesus loves them even when they've made mistakes or been naughty. God's love is unshakable. (Isaiah 54:10)

In this lesson, children will learn that Jesus loves them. Throughout the lesson, remind children of the different aspects of Jesus' love that they have learned so far: He loves us, works miracles for us, feeds us, heals us, forgives us, brings us joy, renews us, and prays for us.

✿ Let's Begin ✿

── Item Needed ──

- Copy of the song "Jesus Loves Me"

1. Sing the song "Jesus Loves Me."

2. Introduce children to the fact that Jesus loves them. Begin by sharing some of the ways you have experienced Jesus' love. Use some of the examples you thought about during your reflection. Then, ask children to think of ways that they have experienced Jesus' love.

✿ Let's Listen ✿

1. Photocopy and cut the *Jesus Loves You* mini-book (pages 87–91) so that you have a set for each child in the class and an extra set for a sample book.

2. Read the *Jesus Loves You* mini-book to the class.

3. Distribute a mini-book to each child. While children are coloring the pages, engage them with the following questions:

- How did Jesus show His love in these stories?

- What did He do for the disciples?

- How does someone show love for you? Share. (After each child has taken a turn and if time allows, let the class have another turn.)

- What ways can we show love to others? (Suggest that children can show love by doing some of the same things that people do for them. Compile a list.)

- Can Jesus show you His love in any of the ways we have listed? Will he use others to show you His love?

JESUS LOVES YOU

CD-204054 • *Jesus Saves! Take-Home Mini-Books*

Children came to see Jesus. The disciples saw the children and started to send them home.
Jesus said, "Let the little children come to me."

Jesus loved the children. Jesus loves you.

2

Jesus went into God's Temple. "This is a house of prayer, not a place for robbers."
Jesus chased away the bad people.
Children shouted, "Hooray for Jesus!"

3

Jesus loved God. Jesus loves you.

4

Jesus pointed to a flock of sheep. "If one of those sheep is lost, the good shepherd will search everywhere for that lost sheep."
A child looked at Jesus. "Would you look for me?"
"I am the good shepherd. I would look for you. I will lay down my life for you."

5

Jesus loved the child. Jesus loves you.

Jesus invited the disciples to dinner. He knelt in front of one man and washed his feet. He knelt in front of another disciple and washed his feet. Jesus washed every disciple's feet.

Jesus loved the disciples. Jesus loves you.

8

❧ Note to Parents ❧

Today, your child learned some of the ways that Jesus shows us His love. Your child has learned some of the ways that she can show love to others. Discuss with your child ways that she can show God's love to others. Encourage your child to follow through with these actions.

Activities for Home

1. Ask your child to give everybody in your family a hug today and tell him that she loves him.

2. Have your child make a card for someone he loves, telling that person that he loves him and that Jesus does, also. Give or mail the card to that person.

3. With your family, sing the song "Jesus Loves Me."

4. Jesus loves you. Read these stories in:
   Matthew 19:13–15, 21:12–16; Luke 15:4–7; John 13:1–12

✤ Let's Create ✤

— Items Needed —

- Copies of the Sheep Pattern (page 93) on white construction paper or card stock

- Scissors and glue

- Cotton balls

- Craft eyes (one per child)

1. Prepare a sheep before class to demonstrate the craft project.

2. Read the parable of the lost sheep in Luke 15:4–7.

3. Distribute copies of the Sheep Pattern (page 93). Place cotton balls, craft eyes, and glue on the table(s) for children to use.

4. Direct children to cut out their sheep. Have precut Sheep Patterns available for children who may have difficulty cutting the Sheep Pattern.

5. Direct children to make their sheep warm and fuzzy by putting the "wool" on it. Show them how to lightly cover the sheep with glue and then place cotton balls on the sheep.

6. Help children glue the craft eyes on the sheep.

Extension Activity

When children have finished making their sheep, have them take turns hiding their sheep in the classroom or outside. The other children will "help Jesus find the lost sheep." Or, bring a wool shawl or costume and let each child take a turn being the sheep while playing Hide-and-Seek.

✤ Let's Puzzle ✤

Photocopy the Lost Sheep worksheet (page 94) for each child. Use in class or as a take-home sheet.

✤ Let's Review and Pray ✤

1. Review with children the list of ways to show love to others.

2. Sing "Jesus Loves Me."

3. Say this prayer:

   Dear Father God, You sent us Your Son because You love us so much. Help us see the many ways that You love us. Thank You. In the name of Your Son, Jesus Christ. Amen.

❧ Sheep Pattern ❧

Jesus Saves! Take-Home Mini-Books • CD-204054

Lost Sheep

Directions: Help Jesus find the lost sheep. Color the sheep hidden in the picture.

"I am the good shepherd. The good shepherd lays down his life for the sheep."

John 10:11

Jesus Suffered for Us
❧ Prepare Your Heart ❧

For God so loved the world that he gave his one and only Son, that whoever believes in him shall not perish but have eternal life. John 3:16

. . . Christ Jesus: Who, being in very nature God, did not consider equality with God something to be grasped, but made himself nothing, taking the very nature of a servant, being made in human likeness. And being found in appearance as a man, he humbled himself and became obedient to death—even death on a cross! Philippians 2:5–8

In this lesson, Jesus' life of healing, teaching, and miracles are culminated with His sacrifice of death on the cross. He paid the ultimate price for our salvation.

Sit quietly and think about your sins. Thank Jesus for the sacrifice He made to have those sins forgiven so that you would have eternal life.

❧ Let's Begin ❧

— Items Needed —
- Easter basket filled with jelly beans
- Song "Christ, the Lord, Is Risen"

1. Ask children, "Who knows which holiday involves celebrating the days in which Jesus died and came back to life?"

2. Hold up an Easter basket filled with jelly beans. "Who knows what this is? During which holiday do we find baskets like these?"

3. Pass around the basket and let each child take some jelly beans. While the basket goes around, sing "Christ, the Lord, Is Risen."

❧ Let's Listen ❧

1. Photocopy and cut the *Jesus Suffered for Us* mini-book (pages 96–100) so that you have a set for each child in the class and an extra set for a sample book.

2. Read the *Jesus Suffered for Us* mini-book to the class.

3. Distribute a mini-book to each child. While children are coloring the pages, engage them with the following questions:

- What does Easter mean? Why do we celebrate this holiday?

- Why did Jesus die on the cross? What does it mean to be saved by Jesus?

- How does your family celebrate Easter?

JESUS SUFFERED FOR US

Pilate asked the crowd, "Shall I let him go?"
The crowd yelled, "Crucify him! Crucify him!"
Pilate ordered Jesus to be whipped. The soldiers placed a crown of thorns on Jesus' head.

Jesus suffered for the crowd. Jesus suffered for you.

Jesus was nailed to the cross. People came to watch. They made fun of Him. Jesus looked at the people making fun of Him. He prayed, "Father, forgive them, for they do not know what they are doing."

Jesus suffered for the people. Jesus suffered for you.

4

At the top of the mountain, the soldiers hung Jesus on the cross.
Jesus cried out to God, "Father, I am coming to You. My work is finished."
The sun stopped shining.

5

Jesus suffered for the people. Jesus suffered for you. **6**

Mary ran to tell the disciples, "Jesus is alive! Christ has risen!" But the disciples did not believe her.
Jesus came into their house. "Look at My hands. Look at My side. Touch Me and see. I am here. I gave My life to save yours." **7**

Jesus suffered for the world. Jesus suffered for you.

8

❧ Note to Parents ❧

In this lesson, Jesus' life of healing, teaching, and miracles are culminated with His sacrifice of death on the cross. Jesus paid the ultimate price for our salvation.

Help your child understand the Easter blessings of Christ's death and resurrection. Help him understand that Jesus suffered because He loves us so much. Talk with your child about what it means to be saved by Jesus.

❧ ❧ ❧ ❧ ❧ ❧

Activities for Home

1. Ask your child what his favorite activities are at Easter.

2. Explain to your child how your family began some of your Easter traditions.

3. Sing Easter songs. In class, your child sang "Christ, the Lord, Is Risen."

4. Jesus suffered for you. Read these stories in:
   Matthew 27:11–26; Luke 23:32–43; John 19:28–37, 20:10–31

❧ Let's Create ❧

— Items Needed —

- Two copies of the Cross Necklace Pattern (page 102) on construction paper or card stock for each child

- Scissors and crayons or felt pens

- Single hole-punch

- Colorful yarn

1. Distribute two copies of the Cross Necklace Pattern (page 102) on construction paper or card stock to each child.

2. Instruct children to decorate and cut out their crosses. Have precut cross patterns available for children who may have difficulty cutting. When they have finished, put the two crosses together and help them punch holes around the edges.

3. Instruct children to weave colorful yarn through the holes. Leave lengths of yarn at the ends to make necklaces.

4. Tell children that the cross will help them remember that Jesus loves them so much that He suffered and died for them.

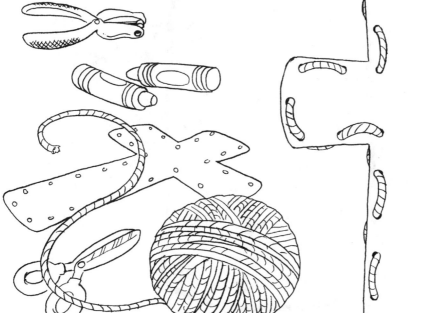

Extension Activity

Retell the stories of Jesus that children have learned throughout these lessons. You can use the cross they made as a prop.

❧ Let's Puzzle ❧

Photocopy the Jesus Suffered for Us worksheet (page 103) for each child. Use in class or as a take-home sheet.

❧ Let's Review and Pray ❧

1. Review the events of Jesus' death and resurrection with children.

2. Remind children that Jesus died for them.

3. Say this prayer:

    Dear Father God, thank You for sending Your Son to suffer and die for our sins. Help us to know You better. In the name of Your Son, Jesus Christ. Amen.

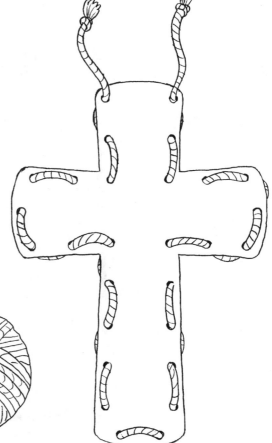

✿ Cross Necklace Pattern ✿

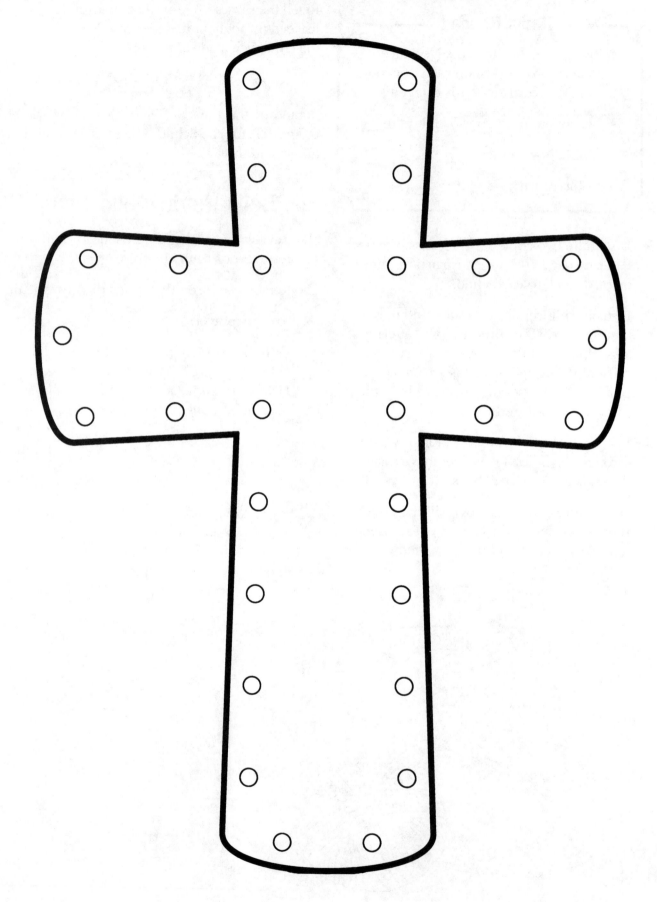

Jesus Suffered for Us

Directions: Follow the maze from Jesus in the garden to the empty tomb.

START

CRACK!

FINISH

"He is not here; he has risen, just as he said."
Matthew 28:6

Jesus Sends the Holy Spirit

✤ Prepare Your Heart ✤

". . . do not worry about . . . what you will say, for the Holy Spirit will teach you at that time what you should say." Luke 12:11–12

May the God of hope fill you with all joy and peace as you trust in him, so that you may overflow with hope by the power of the Holy Spirit. Romans 15:13

As you teach children today, rely on God's promise to fill you with His Spirit. The Holy Spirit will be faithful to God's promise. Sit quietly and close your eyes. Think about the nine fruit of the Spirit (love, joy, peace, patience, kindness, goodness, faithfulness, gentleness, and self-control) and how they are already in you because of the indwelling Holy Spirit. The ones that you practice most will bear the most fruit in your life. Write down times when the fruit of the Holy Spirit has shown in your life. Would any of these be fun to share with children?

✤ Let's Begin ✤

── Items Needed ──

- Copies of the Fruit Patterns (page 111)
- Scissors and felt pens
- Tape or straight pins
- One paper plate

1. Cut a paper plate in half and attach it to a wall or board to make a fruit basket.

2. Cut out the fruit patterns and use a marker to write a quality of the Holy Spirit on each piece of fruit (love, joy, peace, patience, kindness, goodness, faithfulness, gentleness, and self-control.) Distribute the fruit to children. Let them take turns holding up the fruit and putting it in the basket.

3. As each child holds up her fruit, read which fruit of the Spirit it is and give a brief description. Explain that when we allow these fruit to grow in our lives, we are growing more and more like Jesus.

✤ Let's Listen ✤

1. Photocopy and cut the *Jesus Sends the Holy Spirit* mini-book (pages 105–109) so that you have a set for each child in the class and an extra set for a sample book.

2. Read the *Jesus Sends the Holy Spirit* mini-book to the class.

3. Distribute a mini-book to each child. While children are coloring the pages, engage them with the following questions:

- Whom does Jesus promise to send to help us?

- Which fruit of the Spirit can you remember from the basket?

- The Holy Spirit helped Jesus' friends. How can He help you? (comfort, convict, forgive, guide, teach, or help us to say the right things.)

- Have you ever told a lie? Did you feel bad inside or feel like you should have told the truth? That was the Holy Spirit speaking to you.

JESUS SENDS THE HOLY SPIRIT

 CD-204054 • *Jesus Saves! Take-Home Mini-Books*

Jesus said, "Go tell the people that the kingdom of heaven is near."
The disciples said, "But, what shall we say?"
Jesus said, "Do not worry about what to say or how to say it. The Holy Spirit will help you. The Spirit will speak through you."

Jesus promised the Holy Spirit. The Holy Spirit is with you. **2**

The Pharisees pointed at Jesus and said, "You are the prince of demons."
Jesus said, "You can call Me names and be forgiven. But, do not say anything
bad about the Holy Spirit. You cannot be forgiven if you sin against the Holy Spirit." **3**

Jesus promised the Holy Spirit. The Holy Spirit is with you.

Jesus said, "I have much to tell you. When I go to heaven, the Holy Spirit will come and tell you the truth."

The disciples were sad. "We do not want you to go," they said.

"It is good for you that I go. The Holy Spirit will not come unless I go."

Jesus promised the Holy Spirit. The Holy Spirit is with you.

6

Jesus told His disciples, "All authority in Heaven and on Earth has been given to me. Therefore, go and make disciples of all nations, baptizing them in the name of the Father and of the Son and of the Holy Spirit."

7

Jesus promised the Holy Spirit. The Holy Spirit is with you.

8

❧ Note to Parents ❧

Your child learned about the gifts of the Holy Spirit in today's lesson. Galatians 5:22–23 tells us what those gifts are: "But the fruit of the Spirit is love, joy, peace, patience, kindness, goodness, faithfulness, gentleness and self-control. Against such things there is no law."

During the week, help your child recognize the "fruit of the Spirit" showing in her life. Remind your child that God promises that the Holy Spirit will help us whenever asked.

Activities for Home

1. Write down each fruit of the Spirit and beside the word, have your child paste a picture from a magazine that represents that gift. For example, patience can be represented by a picture of a child helping a younger child.

2. Have your child choose a fruit of the Spirit and practice showing that fruit all day. Encourage him to ask the Holy Spirit for help.

3. The Holy Spirit is with you. Read these stories in:
   Matthew 10:7, 19–20, 12:22–32; John 16:5–7; Matthew 28:18–20

✦ Let's Create ✦

Items Needed

- One 9" (22.9 cm) dinner-sized paper plate for each child

- One copy of the Fruit Patterns (page 111) for each child.

- Scissors and crayons or felt pens

1. Cut a dinner-sized paper plate in half to use as a fruit basket.

2. Distribute the Fruit Patterns (page 111) and direct children to use a felt pen to write a fruit of the Holy Spirit on each fruit, color, cut out, and attach to the paper plate. Have precut fruit patterns available for children who may have difficulty cutting.

Extension Activity

Items Needed

- Picture of a large fruit basket on a bulletin board or drawn on the board

- Fruit of the Spirit (page 111) that have already been labeled, decorated, and prepped with tape

- Blindfold

Use the fruit and basket from the Let's Create activity to play *Put the Fruit in the Basket* (similar to *Pin the Tail on the Donkey*).

1. Explain what each fruit is.

2. Blindfold a child and spin her around.

3. Give the child one piece of the fruit and ask her to place the fruit in the basket.

4. Continue until all the fruit is in the basket.

✦ Let's Puzzle ✦

Photocopy the Jesus Sends the Holy Spirit worksheet (page 112) for each child. Use in class or as a take-home sheet.

✦ Let's Review and Pray ✦

1. Remind children of the promise that the Holy Spirit will always help them.

2. Review the fruit of the Spirit. Talk about the fruit of the Holy Spirit that you see in each of their lives.

3. Say this prayer:

   Dear Father God, You promised to send us the Holy Spirit to comfort, teach, and guide us. Thank You for living inside of us. In the name of Your Son, Jesus Christ. Amen.

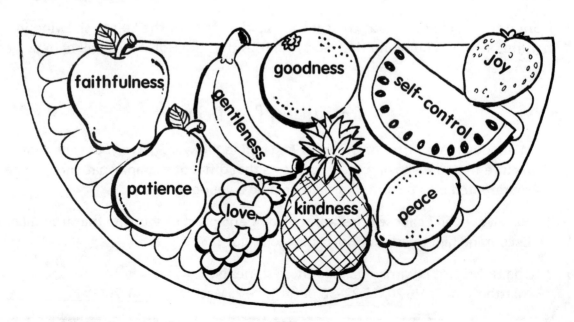

❧ Fruit Patterns ❧

Jesus Sends the Holy Spirit

Directions: Fit the words in the correct spaces to complete the crossword. One letter has been placed for you.

SPIRIT   LOVE   KIND   GENTLE   PEACE

"But when he, the Spirit of truth, comes, he will guide you into all truth."

John 16:13